W9-DFD-985

WITHDRAWN

BLAZERS®

LINE OF DUTY

THE CENTRAL INTELLIGENCE AGENCY

STOPPING TERRORISTS

by Connie Colwell Miller

Content Consultant
Kenneth E. deGraffenreid
Professor of Intelligence Studies
Institute of World Politics
Washington, D.C.

Capstone
press®

Mankato, Minnesota

Blazers are published by Capstone Press,
151 Good Counsel Drive, P.O. Box 669, Mankato, Minnesota 56002.
www.capstonepress.com

Library of Congress Cataloging-in-Publication Data
Miller, Connie Colwell, 1976–
    The Central Intelligence Agency: stopping terrorists / by Connie
Colwell Miller.
    p. cm. — (Blazers. Line of duty)
    Summary: "Describes the CIA, including what it is and what CIA agents
do" — Provided by publisher.
    Includes bibliographical references and index.
    ISBN-13: 978-1-4296-1271-5 (hardcover)
    ISBN-10: 1-4296-1271-1 (hardcover)
    1. United States. Central Intelligence Agency — Juvenile literature.
I. Title. II. Series.
JK468.I6M52 2008
327.1273 — dc22   2007020195

Editorial Credits
Jennifer Besel, editor; Bobbi J. Wyss, designer; Wanda Winch, photo researcher

Photo Credits
AP Photo/Christopher Morris/VII, 15; Damian Dovarganes, 26
Capstone Press/Karon Dubke, 6–7
Corbis/Gabe Palmer, 11; Jeff Rotman, 20; Reuters/Desmond Boylan, 29;
    Reuters/Jason Reed, 8–9; Roger Ressmeyer, 21, 26–27; SABA/Lynsey
    Addario, 14; SYGMA/Larry Downing, 22 (top)
Folio, Inc./Michael Patrick, 4–5
Getty Images Inc./AFP/Tim Sloan, 24; Justin Sullivan, 25; Newsmakers/David
    Burnett, cover; Time & Life Pictures/Wil Blanche, 16–17; U.S. Central
    Command, 22 (bottom)
Landov LLC/Dennis Brack, 19 (bottom)
Shutterstock/Alex Saberi, 12–13; Galina Barskaya, 28; Ursula, 19 (top)

1 2 3 4 5 6 13 12 11 10 09 08

TABLE OF CONTENTS

UNDERCOVER SPIES

Foreign leaders, watch out! Secrets are never safe. Spies for the Central Intelligence Agency (CIA) will uncover hidden plans.

[**foreign** — from another country]

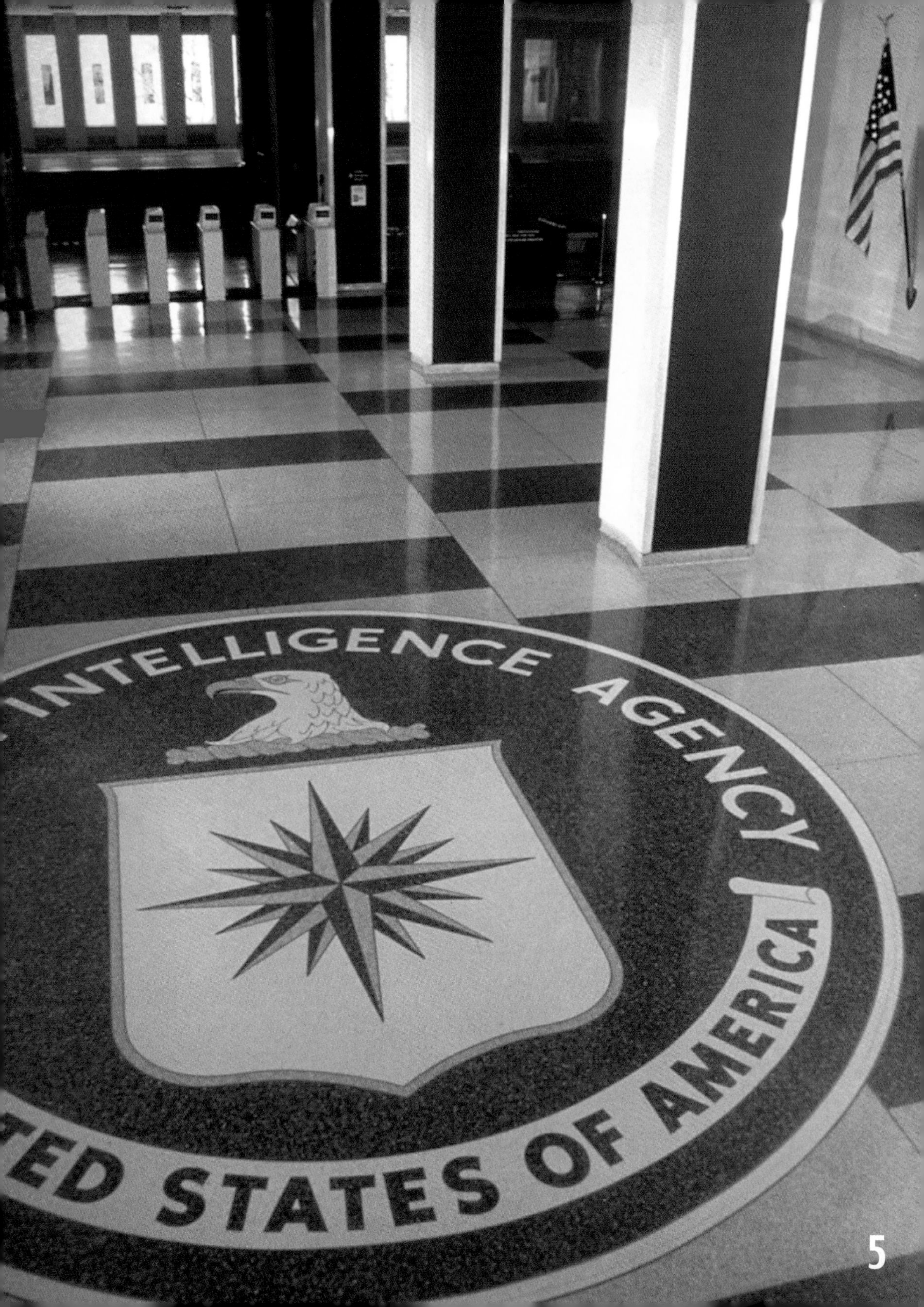
INTELLIGENCE AGENCY
ED STATES OF AMERICA

The CIA works to find out
about threats to U.S. safety.
CIA workers search the
Internet for enemy plans.

FACT! The CIA spies on almost every country — not just the ones we think are dangerous.

7

IN HONOR OF THOSE MEMBERS
OF THE CENTRAL INTELLIGENCE AGENCY
WHO GAVE THEIR LIVES IN THE SERVICE OF THEIR COUN

Each star stands for a spy
who died in the line of duty.

CIA spies work **undercover** in foreign countries. Their job is to steal secrets. They want to find out what others are planning.

[**undercover** — in secret]

FACT! A CIA spy's job is very secret. Often only one other CIA worker knows that spy works for the agency.

GATHERING INFORMATION

CIA spies work inside foreign offices. Spies pay people for information. The information might tell where weapons are stored.

CIA spies get people from other countries to be **agents** for the CIA. The CIA pays agents to share information about their countries' plans.

[**agent** — a person who is hired by a CIA spy to get information about their own country]

FACT! CIA agents take great risks by selling secrets to the United States. They could be put in prison or even killed by their own countries.

Agents work inside **terrorist** groups. They try to learn where these enemies might strike next.

[**terrorist** — someone who uses violence and threats to frighten people]

بعقوبة
2004/1/29

إصابة عدد من رجال الشرطة العراقية
في هجوم على دوريتهم

15

In 1982, the CIA put a virus in some computers to ruin Russia's plans. The virus caused a pipeline to blow up.

CIA spies also give enemies false information. Spies try to confuse enemies and ruin their plans.

FACT!

CIA spies need approval from the president of the United States to go on secret missions.

SECRET-STEALING TOOLS

Spies use equipment to get information. They use hidden cameras to take pictures of documents. Enemies won't know the spies have their secrets.

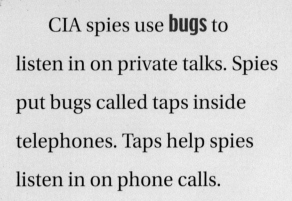

CIA spies use **bugs** to listen in on private talks. Spies put bugs called taps inside telephones. Taps help spies listen in on phone calls.

[**bug** — a hidden microphone]

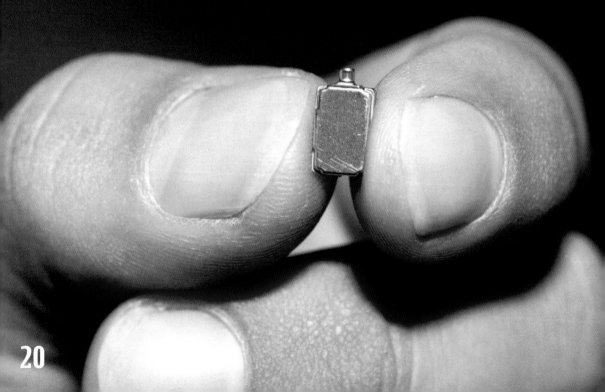

Operations Center at the CIA

Building Pax are
carrying Ammo
to and fro

Mortar Position

Iman Ali Shrine

22

The CIA uses **satellites** to see things in other countries. Satellites take pictures. The pictures might show the size of an enemy's army.

[**satellite** — a spacecraft used to send and receive information]

FACT! Satellites can zoom in very close. CIA workers can see how many airplanes an enemy has at a base.

Spies often use makeup or fake body parts to make themselves look different.

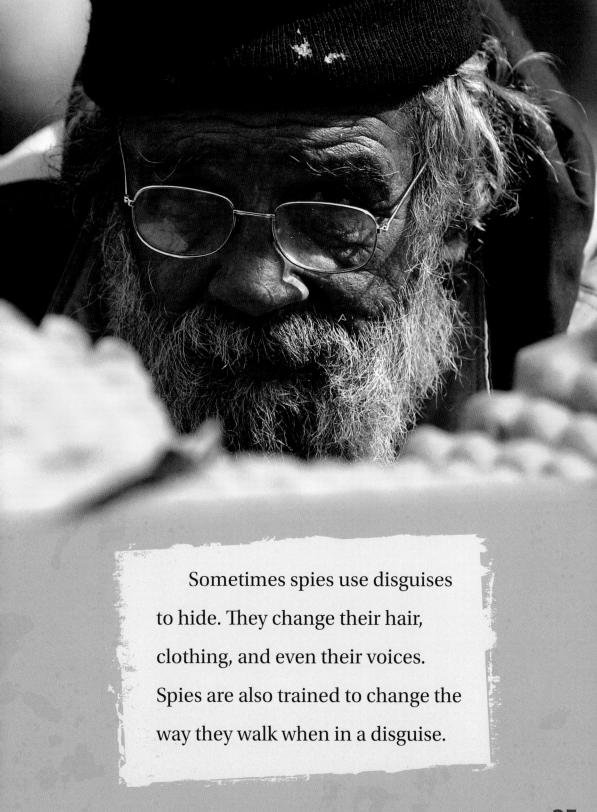

Sometimes spies use disguises to hide. They change their hair, clothing, and even their voices. Spies are also trained to change the way they walk when in a disguise.

SHARING INFORMATION

CIA workers study the spies' information. They share terrorist plans with the president. The president has to decide what to do.

FACT! The CIA prepares an update for the president every morning. It is called the President's Daily Brief.

The President's Daily Briefing
President Bush

TOP SECRET

former CIA director
William Webster

CIA spies hide around the world. They steal enemy secrets. The information they find keeps our country safe.

29

GLOSSARY

agent (AY-jent) — a foreign spy for the CIA

bug (BUHG) — a hidden microphone

foreign (FOR-uhn) — from another country

satellite (SAT-uh-lite) — a spacecraft used to send signals and information from one place to another

terrorist (TER-ur-ist) — someone who uses violence and threats to frighten people

undercover (uhn-dur-KUHV-ur) — done in secret

READ MORE

Abraham, Philip. *The CIA*. Top Secret. New York: Children's Press, 2003.

Hamilton, John. *The CIA*. Defending the Nation. Edina, Minn.: Abdo, 2007.

INTERNET SITES

FactHound offers a safe, fun way to find Internet sites related to this book. All of the sites on FactHound have been researched by our staff.

Here's how:
1. Visit *www.facthound.com*
2. Choose your grade level.
3. Type in this special code **1429612711** for age-appropriate sites. You may also browse subjects by clicking on letters, or by clicking on pictures or words.
4. Click on the **Fetch It** button.

FactHound will fetch the best sites for you!

INDEX